Imagine

Imagine　Nothing　　　Imagine　Creation

Imagine　Earth　　　Imagine　A human being

By Tom Fallon

Through A Stranger's Eyes

The Man On The Moon

In The First Place

New Pennacook Poetry Series

NOW - Works on Paper 1976-2010

Creation Now With Words

Imagine

Tom Fallon

Imagine   Copyright © 2023   Thomas C. Fallon, Jr.

All rights reserved. No part of this book may be reproduced in any form without written permission of the author. However, reviewers may quote brief passages in a review to be published in a newspaper, magazine or literary journal.

ISBN: 978-1-59713-280-0

Library of Congress Control Number: 2023941350

Printed for Transition Books by
Goose River Press
3400 Friendship Road
Waldoboro Maine 04572-6337

Cover design by Lindy Gifford of *Manifest Identity*

To the Seven

Where do we come from? What are we? Where are we going?

> Paul Gaugin

I am only interested in the relations between man and God.

> Eugene O'Neill

Contents

Author Note

Silence

Naked   ocean waves break on white sand

Presence   in   to

Imagine   naked she said   " i am alive "

Silence

Author Note

Imagine Creation exists - space, silence, time, exist - in Creation imagine created forms exist charged moving wild - imagine intelligence, and self-consciousness, of the human being, in the great Creation.

Space, silence, time,
first presented to the author in Anton Webern's *Opus 7 for violin and piano* &
live creation presented by
Thelonious Monk's comping behind soloists leading to his wild solo
in *Well, You Needn't* at the '61 Amsterdam stint!

IMAGINE is a four part prose and free verse literary form of the incredible creation, beautiful and frightening, for human beings. Part one, *Naked,* presents the darkness, danger, violence, the threat in creation while in part two, *Presence,* the human relation to and the necessity for, a creator, exists. Three, *Imag*ine, has the beauty, joy and wildness with intelligence and self awareness of the questioning human being leading to part four, the *Silence,* the possible future of the incredible and mysterious great creation.

Now

Tom Fallon

Silence

imagine

nothing

silence

imagine

movement

creation

time

space

earth

sun light

imagine

a multiplicity of life forms

a human being

imagine

beauty

warmth

love

imagine

Naked

ocean   waves   break   on   white sand

a human being standing					sun set

					waves break slowly on white sand

		alone

			stephen

						fire red yellow orange sky

stephen walking slowly on white sand

		thinking

					i exist			*i will die*

i will cease to exist on this earth		*my body rot crumble to dust*

						i die

                                                             i do not know   if i will exist   in spiritual form   conscious   in another place

            in heaven   *or hell*

                                                                                      i do not know

i exist on earth now   *in the universe*   *in creation*   *here*

                                                                                       stephen stopped walking

                              why do I exist

                                                        picked up a small stone throwing it into the slow breaking waves

                walk slowly on the white sand

gone   *into the silence of eternity*   *nothingness*   *into oblivion*

                                            murdered   *by God the creator*   *in pain*   *suffering*   *dead*

              ive seen the pain and horror of life   *covering news of the world for the times ive been at the wars   in the wars   the revolutions   the raping of women and young girls, bayonetting of children, beheading of fathers, old men*

the senseless murder, the rage

it is unimaginable

*ive been at earthquakes   seen the ravaging of hunger and disease plaques   starvation during droughts   the unbelievable devastation of tornados
floods, volcanos wiping out villages and cities   ive even seen the devastation of a meteor*

ive seen children starving, lying in their dead mother's arms

ive seen lynchings of blacks in the American south   my own uncle

stephen slowly walking   waves breaking slowly on the white sand

fire red yellow orange sky

ive covered genocides around the world   the destruction of a civilization, the original "americans"

ive seen the pain and suffering and ugliness of death   so many human beings suffered who did not deserve such death at the hands of other human beings

the madness of humanity   and i   i   will die

ive seen the violent death of animals   the same as the violent death of human beings, over and over and over

human bodies floating in saltwater bays after a typhoon   *unnamed uncounted human beings thrown into mass graves*

there are no words to truly describe such inhuman violence

in cities women and children raped and starving, children selling their bodies on streets for food   *ive seen millionaires thriving*

i heard the crying of helpless hunan beings

ive cried   yes, ive cried

ive seen civilized human beings smile, shake hands   deceive and lie   pimp and whore   intimidate and enslave   yes, kill   kill other human beings

for the good of society   for personal gain   for power, and money

ive seen a people, a nation, managed by their technology

fire red yellow orange sky darkening

stephen stopped   slowly shaking his head   tears in his eyes

ive asked for a reason for this violence   such anger, such hate   such relentless cruelty   ive been given no reason yes, ive asked God

nothing   no answer

stephen stopped in the white sand

i wrote the news, printed in black words   *words of rage and murder every day, every week, every month, every year*   *no blood on the news page*   *no pain*

after death of a human being   there is no communication   no human words   silence

unending silence

the horror of life is real   the agony of human beings is real

day after day, year after year, century after century on earth

stephen slowly walking   waves break slowly on the white sand

he stopped

                picked up a small stone   throws the stone into the slow breaking waves

walking slowly

                          why do I exist   *to die*

                                                                        why do we exist

i must have some meaning   *we must have some meaning*

                                                creation must have some meaning

                    God   *I ask you*   *why the senseless rage, murder*   *endlessly*

                                                                                                                   why

waves breaking slowly on white sand

                                                              stephen   alone   slowly walking

                                                sky dark

                                        picks up another stone   throws the stone into the slowly breaking waves

            slowly walks in the dark

                                                    air warm

    low sound of thunder in the distance   stephen stopped walking

                                        where is God

                                                                waves break slowly on the white sand

                            sky dark

i have not seen God   *i have not heard God speak*

                            stephen slowly sits in the sand

waves break slowly on the white sand

warm air

"I exist," stephen said   surprised by his voice

"I will die," he said.

waves break slowly on the white sand

the air warm

ocean

she died

ocean

stephen stood

walked slowly into the breaking waves

God does not exist

he laughed quietly

waves break slowly on the white sand

Jesus did not have to die

silence

stephen disappeared

silence

Presence

in   to

Have you ever sensed that our soul is
immortal and never dies?

                                        Plato

young

alone

a room

thought

I know you are here

I know you'll hear me

I haven't succeeded

                                              I know that you know

                                                  I have to say it
                                                    for myself

I sense I have eight years now   Is it true

                                     You told me fifty two years ago

                                            The time

I am close

                                                                                   And they are nervous

                                                                                         as you warned me

They are more nervous now

                                                                                                     I see

                                             As I move closer

             There is danger as you told me
                      in the beginning

When you touched me   you gave me no choice

I moved away   and I was alone

They watched me as they
had watched others

                                                                                         I moved quietly

You, there

                                        I knew I wasn't alone

Always your encouragement,
your touch, our conversation

Living

I have been afraid

                                                                        When you disappeared

I know you warned me about the silence

                                        But it was deafening

                                                                        At times, a horror

There is no other word for it

Silence

Your non existence

I was able to stay,
trembling, alone

You are here now					I stand

I know creation is my place as it is yours

                I knew you were there, here, somewhere

                                      I was alone

                                      I was not alone

And now the final eight years

Yes, I laugh

Because you are here

Knowing the future
as they watch in fear

I am one   Not alone

I am alive

I am alone   I am not alone

Now

They are coming   I can hear them

What do you want me to do

"Talk with them"

"Now"

Stopping on the path through woods
under the colored leaves

"i am with you"

Imagine

naked she said   " i am alive "

Urge and urge and urge,
Always the procreant urge of the world.

                Walt Whitman

Inebriate of air — am I —
And Debouchee of Dew —
Reeling — thro' Endless Summer Days —
From inns of Molten Blue —

                Emily Dickinson

imagine

                                                              sun shining bright

                   a green leafed maple tree

a field of wild green grasses and coloring wildflowers

                                   birds singing in the trees surrounding the field

                                              a hawk flying quick over the field and away

            a doe, with two young, slowly crossing the field

                            quiet flowing brook

imagine

loreen

young loreen rose naked from bed and stood in the sunlight flooding the room from the window

said quietly into the sun warming room   "i am alive"

she rubbed her face and her shoulders, her arms and breasts, her stomach, her pubis, her thighs and calves, and feet

she stretched her young naked body slowly upward, her arms high above herself into the sun light

"i am alive" she said slowly, quietly, smiling, closing her eyes

"i am alive," she said clearly

she laughed, and danced in the sun light

john

young john woke in the shed to the summer sun rising over the field of wild green grasses and coloring wildflowers he had built the shed to create after graduating since painting would have been difficult with his artist friends so often focused on drinking and the night life   he wanted only to create   the birds were quietly singing in the trees which surrounded the field   he saw a doe with two young slowly crossing the field   a hawk flew over the field and away, returned again and flew away again   he heard the slow flowing of the brook hidden in the trees surrounding the field   he thought *paradise this is my paradise   i am free free to create*   naked, he stood, stretched, left the shed and walked into the field in sun light john remembered meeting loreen   on a day he walked into town to replenish his paints

i approached a young woman walking toward me on the sidewalk   i didn't know her and had never seen her before
          i naturally looked into her eyes as he approached her   and i stopped walking
she stopped when i stopped   her eyes had stopped me   irrationally i didn't, couldn't, look away from her eyes
she looked into my eyes   i didn't speak at first   she didn't speak   she was beautiful but it was her eyes which held me
          finally, feeling absurd, i asked if i could meet her somewhere   she said yes quietly
     we met a week later   we met in the town park and i couldn't stop talking   she didn't speak a word
she listened   loreen was her name, she said   i was confused because she was silent and finally said I'll see you later
          i returned to the field confused
     she wouldn't leave my mind   her eyes   her eyes wouldn't leave my mind   i was mesmerized

a week after our meeting in town she walked to the field to visit me   I was stunned   we talked then   she talked, then
     we began to relate to each other naturally   she was eighteen and i was twenty three   she was so young
     and she returned another time to the field to visit me   i became more comfortable with her   and she was warmer
     she visited me a third time and she said that she would stay with me   I said we would have to live in the shed
          she said yes   we lived in the shed
     so our journey together began   and i continued creating, painting

imagine

the summer sun shining warm

we lay naked in the summer grass

her skin is light orange in color but her light brown freckles made her orange color shimmer in my eyes

the flickering white and yellow light of the sun and moving white clouds intensified her shimmering orange color

i lay about a foot from her in the grass

she had closed her eyes   and was smiling

we were quiet in the light

the sun shining on her arm, the hair of her forearm feathery in the sun light

i looked at the hair on her forearm in the light

i reached toward her arm hair

i ran my fingers slowly just over the top of the hair

she didn't move

loreen is so alive   i thought   *so alive*

i woke in the shed and saw loreen running naked rain poring out of the sky dancing in the field around
the maple tree shouting "I am alive, I am created, I am creation," running back into the house and
stopping in front of me embracing me with both her arms saying breathlessly "i am alive,"
shouting "i am alive, i love you jonny," standing away from me spreading her arms wide
joy flashing in her eyes breathlessly whispering "I am alive I am alive I am alive jonny, I love you,"
I in shock laughing she embracing me fiercely

we're building a house in the field together

one day at a time it is and naturally loreen is pregnant now

we've worked on the house for a year we're adding a studio for painting

our child will be born next summer

we'll marry in the house after it's completed

we love each other with passion living in this paradise

loving, working, creating

one day loreen added a little white dog to our life

she named him amady, amadeus after mozart, who follows us everywhere i began to change with loreen and baby jonny, creating abstract stronger energy in new forms more easily while painting

i was surprised by my increased energy

life in the house our life was alive in a way i had never known in my life

i turned away from previous forms i'd relied on without a thought

i became aware of the natural growth in the fields and woods around us and began to abstract new form from there

everything came to me in a rush, an explosion, of creation, painting

i suddenly had confidence in my new direction even diverging from the direction of a previous painting

i felt happier, lighter, as a human being as well as i finished paintings at an amazing clip

i was exhilarated by this new force which had charged my creating now carrying me when creating one painting after another

even amady the little dog energized me to laughter which was a freedom i'd never before experienced

so i was now creating with freedom

at times loreen would walk slowly in the sun light   moving in the field   little jonny in her arms   very slowly   slowly

dancing   slowly   naked she was   she was unafraid of her body   her flesh   singing softly   i could barely hear her

moving very slowly though the sun light, the grasses, the wildflowers of the field   softly singing   she not quite here, in another world mother and child

loreen and jonny in the sun

in the wild green grasses and coloring wildflowers of the field

jonny   the child   suddenly running   in the field

loreen with a red ball

loreen   with jonny   "throw it throw it mama"

loreen throwing the red ball into the air

little jonny running   the child giggling   chasing the ball flying in the air above him

catching the ball   giggling   laughing aloud   circling the maple tree

"throw it throw it jonny"   loreen calling running   laughing   chasing the red ball flying the air

missing the ball loreen falling rolling over in the grass and wildflowers laughing

little jonny falling into the grass giggling laughing beside her

mother and child   happy

playing, laughing

one early morning when i went to the studio i found a canvas on the easel with words in created in pencil

one morning i came to the studio i noted i was slowly introducing light, at times bright, colors, into my abstract style paintings   also replacing my favored straight and jagged lines with curved lines and circles   i hadn't noticed this before   i took out earlier paintings to see where my creations may have changed   it had changed there was no doubt   i discovered the paintings began to slowly change after i met loreen   change quickening after we were married, living closely together   light, bright colors   curved lines and circles   appeared and multiplied   in one painting i discovered an obvious sun   i had never seen this "sun" before   it was realistic in the otherwise abstract style painting   loreen   loreen had affected me with her beauty   her life force   so real to me present   she possessing an unusual radiance   spiritual maybe, i thought   transcendent beauty?   her reality   her body   real   she unlike any person i'd ever known   and nothing that i as an artist had imagined creating   her beauty, one could say, i might say, came from another world   i have sensed this myself often in her presence   no, no, she is a woman   a human being, no mystery   irrational, real, as i am   this is absurd   no   paint   create, i said aloud   stop what are you thinking, paint   it's absurd   i was uncertain   i continued painting, creating, but i did not leave the vibrant colors and new line forms   i painted   she was human i continued in the abstract direction natural for me   loreen   was real, that was the problem stop thinking this way   the bright colors continued to appear on the canvas   i could not stop this from happening   why was she affecting me this way   i must create what i am   now

i sense

i feel

i taste

i hear

i see

i smell

i act

i think

i imagine

i fear

i cry

i bleed

i laugh

i love

i am

imagine

morning   in the studio   jon   looking   out   into   the   field   to the maple tree

light   spring   rain   slowly   falling   to   the   field

leaves   of   the   maple tree   moving   slowly

he   watched   the rain   fall

we sat together on the porch of the house

the moon was full

we listening to the crickets in the field

loreen slowly ran her finger up her arm

"i am warm." she whispered to me

"feel my arm," she whispered

i moved two fingers slowly up her arm

she was warm

she felt my arm slowly with her fingers

"you're warm," she whispered

"warm," she whispered, her fingers touching my arm

i shivered

i would wake at night   hearing loreen's voice   she whispering   "i am alive"   two, three times   then nothing

when i woke the sun light was shining into the room   loreen was asleep beside me as usual and lay naked in the sun light
jonny came into the room and jumped up on the bed to wake her   she woke laughing tickled him and they fell on the floor

"daddy! i got the red ball - come play with me," johnny shouting outside the studio and I turned from painting to see him in the field bouncing the red ball off the door, throwing it into the air, laughing with amady circling at his feet "i'll play" i called to him running out of the studio to catch the red ball as he threw it to me i throwing it back to him and he caught the ball quickly throwing it into the air away from me so i had to run to catch it, he laughing, shouting, jumping, clapping his hands with joy, amady running into the field with us i laughing, clapping, calling "whoopie johnny" throwing the red ball into the air running as happy and innocent as any child could be

her eyes   i would look into them   or she would look at me   we would connect   i was mesmerized by her   i would stop painting snow falling   the air cold, crisp, clean   so, winter   everything in the field white with snow the maple tree unleafed

sitting on the front porch   amady in my lap, i slowly stroking the little dog's fur   jonny sitting in his small chair next to me

"i remember the first snowfall of each year, jonny   the first snowfall of the year always seems to fall very very slowly

"small snow flakes very slowly falling   not big flakes   and it always seems the snow is a present to us

"the snowflakes, the snow, storm, so beautiful, jonny   loreen and i would stand out in the snow and listen to it fall around us and on us

"there was no sound at all when the snow landed on us it seemed   the snow flakes were so light, so light, landing on us

"and sometimes loreen and i would run and play in the snow like kids   you know, someone your age

"loreen and i love the beauty of falling snow, john,"

i stopped speaking   watching the white snow flakes falling so slowly   seeing

white   *falling*   *silently*   *beauty*   *a serenity*   *snow*   *white*   *every where*   *every where*

i watched the snow   *taking in the soundless*   *slow falling*   *snow*   *flakes*

one day loreen came into the studio when i was painting and when i turned to her she said with an unusual fierceness

you create   *you are an artist, a painter*   *you are a create   the energy of creation, from the creator, is within you*

you draw from the real creation source, the creator, the source of creation, to paint, to create   so you are alive and create

you live with that tremendous force, in and of and from creation, from the creator, the source, the universe, creation

it is the rule of creation   you create and you destroy and create and destroy as the creator does   you create life, real creations john

you must continue to paint, create, from life, the source, real beauty, john, life   creation   she said loudly and she left

i was stunned   you must paint creation, life, love, real beauty, john, life   i was confused   i was a creator she said

i am as a painter, yes   she connected me directly to the creator of the universe   no, i did not believe, think, this way

the creator exists she said   maybe   i am connected she said to, in, the, a, creator, of the universe

i a poor creature, painter, so connected   we existentialists do not think so   she is unique i know but   maybe a creator does exist

no, no   i was disturbed by her speaking so   i am only a human being   a simple painter   i did not understand her

i love her but   i believed in her unique being, as a creation, yes   herself unique, her life, her love, beauty   no

i stopped painting for a week, confused, disturbed   i sensed she knew some things i did not, yes, but this, this was beyond me loreen lying naked in the field slowly running her hands through the grasses feeling earth under the grasses rolling her body over in the grasses feeling the earth

loreen lying naked in the field slowly running her hands through the grasses feeling earth under the grasses rolling her body over in the grasses feeling the earth

loreen lying naked in the field slowly running her hands through the grasses feeling earth under the grasses rolling her body over in the grasses feeling the earth imagine

           loreen would bite into a ripe peach

              and peach juice would squirt into her face

        and she would laugh ecstatically

licking the peach juice running down her face calling out

      "i love peach, I love peach, the juice, the juice, the juice"

     dancing in circles and biting again into the peach   juice squirting into her face

shouting happily as the peach juice squirted into her face licking the peach juice running down her face and

        dancing with joy and calling out "yes, yes, yes" ecstatically

      dancing in circles around the birch tree

       and she would bite into the peach time after time and dance and dance

   shouting, yes shouting   laughing   laughing   almost wild

SHOUTING "JOY TO PEACH JUICE, JOY TO PEACH JUICE"   shouting shouting happily   laughing   and   dancing

and i, i laughing, yes, i, clapping my hands, yes, i moving myself, my body, around as in a primitive dance, laughing with her, yes

              and we danced! and danced and danced

    shouting JOY, JOY, JOY TO LIFE, LIFE laughing   wild   YES   YES shouting JOY TO CREATION !

loreen lay hidden in the grasses and wildflowers of the field			she thought

				i am alive		*i am a creation*		*which connects me to a, the, creator*

my consciousness created, from someone in creation			*similar in some way to me*			*a creation*

							so, someone, a creator, exists

how, why, does, the creator, in creation, exist *how is the creator created*		*i do not know*		*i have not been told*

	nothing in creation comes from nothing		*i know that*		*everyone knows*		*a creation is from a creation*

		but		*there is pain*		*death*		*disappearance*		*in creation*		*which destroys a creation, creations*

		i do not know why		*why am i created*		*i ask*		*where do i, we*		*yes, you, too, come from*

.	*you clearly spoke to me one time in the past*		*so i am real*		*and, you. you are real*		*i know you are real*		*i know that but no more*

	i have seen beauty		*here*		*i have known warmth*		*i love*		*i love, in reality, here*		*in matter, creation*

				with beauty, love, i do not think i am meaningless			*creation, meaningless*

		speak to me			*now*		*i am here*		*i will not stop asking*			*silence*		she lay in the grass

closed her eyes					*i am alive*				she heard nothing

	she lay still in the grass

one spring night i remember a full moon shining as loreen and i were walking slowly in the field holding hands

she turned to me and said quietly

"i love you"

i turned to her and pursed my lips

she kissed me as a child would and laughed

"again," she said, with joy

we kissed again

"again," she whispered

and we kissed again and we both laughed and we hugged

we were happy

the painting for the exhibition is hell for me   i was so often confused   painting, repainting, again and again, uncertainty in my mind

not about the desire to conform to the committee, to win, but to create as i needed to create   time after time i changed direction   even burning canvases

he lifted the paintbrush in the air

did not touch canvas

jerked hand away

stepped quietly away

eyes on the canvas with red

moved forward slowly

slapped violently on

stopped suddenly

hand with brush in air

stepping very slowly back into the room

farther away   mind fixed on space

he screamed   wild

i fiercely finished the painting for the modern's exhibition   it had been very difficult   speak of birthing a child
i'd finished it more than one time   then made one change, leading to other changes, creating at times an absurdity for me
yes, i continued with the bright colors and curved lines and circles i'd begun to introduce in my paintings
then i was suddenly discouraged by the finished painting   upset, i burned it since I had so many over paintings
the day i burned it outside the studio loreen came
loreen asked me if i was going to continue creating   i didn't reply to her but asked myself what was the matter with her
she said as i turned away from her that i must not stop creating and then left me with the burning painting
i shouted to her to keep away from me when i was creating   i returned to create another painting but did not know what direction
i was disturbed marianne had connected with my creating   i was having difficulty now   and i was disturbed
one day a sun appeared on the canvas as it had earlier   i did not want a sun   i stopped painting for a week disturbed
i returned, rested, somewhat confused, moving slowly away from abstract creating   i did not want lines and circles now
i could not turn away from the sun i had painted   slowly, very slowly, i grew life, beauty, and love, on the canvas
it was absurd   i could now stop this direction   today's art establishment will turn away i knew   but creation, only creation
i was confused and astonished but opened myself to continue creating   and a nude appeared in the sun light
loreen did not pose   a human being   it was not loreen   it was loreen   i created wild without thought

the spring breeze slowly moved the budding limbs of the maple tree in the field johnny sat on the studio floor with paper and pencil slowly making words

john sat down on the floor beside him and asked him what he was doing

"making words" the boy said smiling

"loreen made words and she said I could copy her words if i wanted to"

"look, look at my words, dad" he said raising the paper to john

"listen to the words - see, hear, taste, touch, smell" he said very slowly

"these words - think, feel, imagine - but i don't understand those words so well"

"i understand love though - look - that word there - love" he said with pride showing him the word

"i can make words now all by myself, dad" he said with pride, happy, smiling wide

"and loreen told me all these words were life words"

"true, johnny, true - loreen would know" john said

"i'm alive daddy, just like loreen' he said waving the worded paper around in the air

john hugged his son to his chest happy

johnny smiled, laughing happily

i took the painting to the modern's exhibition committee and

the committee rejected the painting for the exhibition because it did not follow

the committee's guidelines i myself had verbally accepted and print signed   i smiled, thanked the committee for the opportunity

they had presented to me, and returned home   i laughed on the way home

i continue to create   whether institutions accepted me or not

i am a creator   as loreen said clearly   in the universe

i am a creator   i am connected to the creator   to the creative source   force   she. i, connected to the creator of creation

i draw on the source of creation to live and to create

i did not believe, think, know, this at one time

i began to slowly explore different directions now that i was freed from the compulsion to conform to the status quo of the art establishment

imagine

from the studio i heard loreen bouncing the red ball off the walls in the house

suddenly she was running into the field shouting to me "johnny" i ran from the studio into the spring sun light to meet her and johnny ran from the house to meet us with amady bounding and barking after him

we three entered the pale green grass and early wildflowers shedding our clothes because loreen was naked running

shouting and laughing joyously and throwing the red ball into the air at me and i threw it to johnny

    suddenly we were so alive   we felt life rising in us overflowing as we ran wild

    amady barking running with us   life on our earth for us real   surreal   with loreen

    astonishingly real which didn't make sense but we didn't judge as we ran so fully charged alive

naked in the field   loreen   johnny   i   living   young   alive in paradise   our paradise

    loreen leading us in life   she so full   her color   radiance   her vibrating life color

    oh the beauty of her   her beauty   such wild free beauty   her color   her orange

    after time in the sun her freckles intensifying her vitality   her life color vibrating in my eyes

    yes yes yes

she so antithetical to my black and white however energetic mind   so perfect, so living   so miracle it seemed

    amady running and barking with her   as i tossed the ball to johnny and he tossed the ball to loreen

    one would think God existed with such beauty, such life

    around the maple tree

laughter in the sun light of earth   we three naked human beings running and shouting life joy   liberated

loreen throwing the red ball into the air to me   i throwing the ball into the air to johnny

johnny throwing the ball to amady who picked it up and ran alongside loreen picking ball from his mouth

amady running and barking in joy   amady dancing   we three primitives in the sun

we three pitching the red ball into the air and laughing as we tan together in freedom of children naked   at home in life, in life, in life

loreen running into the woods surrounding the field to the stream splashing into the stream and running into the field laughing with joy

so free, so alive, so transcendent so wild   the summer sun warm, warm, rainbow over all

we were alive   we were alive   we were alive

shouting   life, life alive alive in the wild world, creation   the red ball in the air laughing laughing

loreen fell to the grasses and wildflowers laughing and johnny and i fell as well

and then loreen turned to johnny and i wrapping her arms around us we fell to the ground and she said *i am alive, i love you, i love you*

"yes, i love you"   she said   " i love you"   we laughing happily, laughing like fools

we walking slowly back to the house very tired holding hands laughing   amady dancing   we laughing

Silence

i m a g i n e

silence

there are no human beings

no earth

there are no galaxies

no creation

no time

there is nothing

BIO

Tom Fallon w *Through a Stranger's Eyes*, 1978, *The Man on the Moon, The Change of the Century*, 1987, *NOW, Works on Paper, 1976-2006, Poetry and Antipoverty*, 2007, *Creation NowWith Words*, 2020, experiment w literary form, no traditional poetry form.

As a child w meltdowns also running streets burning fields Brockton Massachusetts resist 1st grade school discipline & teacher Berenice Stevenson separate him fr classmates to color rabbit outline. Family move to Auburn Maine, Rumford Maine, continue best school artist & sophomore create sports cartoons for small town newspaper. Boredom high school English visit public library discover *Men of Art* by Thomas Craven stimulated by great art revolution of late 19th early 20th Century.

Late Fifties drop out Rhode of Island School of Design & St. Johns College Annapolis Maryland enlist US Air Force station outside outside New York City Mitchell Air Force Base checked out Ezra Pound's *ABC of Reading* NYC library branch leading to create w words at primitive level, view foreign films Ingmar Bergman, Akira Kurosawa others rundown theater off base, marry & divorce.

Experience nervous breakdown w period in mental hospital begins somewhat stable life direction Rumford Maine town part time jobs continue create primitive writing, (why do I exist) marry 1960 religious girl Maine support uneven temperament & writing.

Discover early Maine Writers & Publishers Alliance support of Lee Sharkey, Mark Melnicove, Constance Hunting encourage explore literary form w complete freedom. Publish in various college & independent literary magazines participate in wild MWPA readings, poetry editor Maine *Times* independent liberal newspaper, drama *A Dying Animal* staged Atma Theater Boston w "Pregnant Man 1" publish w Red Dust NYC & 1st book *Through A Strangers Eyes* w MWPA.

Sixties Seventies visiting New York City exposed wild happenings movement Off Off Broadway theater Cafe Cino, La Mama ETC, Judson Poets Theater w LeRoi Jones, Sam Shepard, Rosalyn Drexler, Jean Claude van Itallie, find modern jazz Thelonious Monk, John Coltrane, Sonny Rollins, Charlie Mingus, Cecil Taylor, Anthony Braxton experimental classical music John Cage, Steve Reich, Philip Glass, George Crumb, Charles Ives &c

Marianne Moore Donald Hall *Paris Review* "I disliked the term *poetry* for any but Chaucer's or Shakespeare's or Dante's. I do not now feel quite my original hostility to the word since it is a convenient almost unavoidable term for the thing (although hardly for me - my observations, experiments in rhythm or exercises in composition). What I write, as I said before, could only be called poetry because there is no other category in which to put it." Word creation. *NOW, Works on Paper, 1976-2006, Poetry and Antipoetry*.

Writers through years - Shakespeare, Keats - Walt Whitman open psyche & literary - Emily Dickinson, Ezra Pound, Hart Crane's *The Bridge*, William Carlos Williams' *Paterson*, Marianne Moore, Charles Olson, e. e. cummings, Dick Higgins, individuals &c.

www.ingramcontent.com/pod-product-compliance
Lightning Source LLC
Chambersburg PA
CBHW041644070526
44586CB00004B/70